OFFERTA
2 KILI
x
€ 3,50

A SCELTA

A SCE

MAGLIA
DI LANA
OFFERTA!!!

€ 6.00

BREAKING CONSTRAINTS

"But Pictor the tree, on the other hand, was always the same, he could not change any more. As soon as he realised this, his happiness vanished: he started growing old and constantly had that tired, serious and afflicted look you see on lots of old trees. You can also see it every day on horses, birds, people and all beings: when they lose the gift of being able to change they gradually sink into sadness and depression and lose all trace of beauty."
Hermann Hesse, *Pictor's Metamorphoses*

Young people ambitious to change the world and unhinge the rules holding it together, enjoying poking fun at it a little, respectfully but bravely, even daring to bring about "revolutions", but "without anybody actually noticing", as the master Bruno Munari would have pointed out with a smile. And as our King Midas of communication and design, who would really be at home here with these people, would have said, the healthy rule that now needs to be applied much more often and with greater clarity is that of breaking them (the rules) in order to move beyond them.

The man who theorised about "breaking constraints" to achieve unexpected results and open up, to discover fresh horizons along paths usually just followed automatically: like that day when using, by way of a machine designed and programmed to reproduce an unlimited number of identical copies of an original (i.e. a photocopier), he managed to obtain originals and not copies (his "original xerographies", a top-shelf oxymoron) and hence unique pieces produced by a machine, showing everybody that ignoring constraints can be a healthy way of avoiding the obvious, actually defeating it; or like that time with the "La regola e il caso" (Rules and Randomness) fabric collections, where an irregular shower of coloured dies dyes freely "soiled" rolls of carefully pre-printed cloths.

Rules and randomness indeed, combining to tell us of rigour and acceleration, method and lateral-thinking. Many years earlier, the same man brought out a little children's book ("Le macchine di Munari" – Munari's Machines) full of acrobatic wordplay ("Attenzione attenzione" – Careful Careful) with a word from each previous line being changed on every new line, creating unlikely puns and paradoxes until reaching the end of a long column and almost restoring order, even after such an inebriating journey, although actually arriving at the exact opposite: "È vietato l'ingresso ai non addetti al lavoro/È vietato il lavoro ai non addetti all'ingresso/È ingrassato l'addetto ai non vietati al lavoro/(...)/ È dettato il permesso ai verdetti del foro/È vietato l'ingresso agli addetti al lavoro (Starting with the Italian for "No entry for unauthorised staff" and then changing one word in every subsequent line you eventually get the Italian for "No entry for authorised staff"). An "exercise in style", as Raymond Queneau would have taught us in his variations on a theme, perceptively translated over into Italian by a certain Umberto Eco.

Transgress to change and improve, setting new records.

So everything can change; and everything needs to change; everything ought to have the healthy capacity to adapt to our times. Flickering and shimmering, reinforcing the changing needs of a period whose temperature is very unsettled: our age.

Daring to break the constraints.

Beppe Finessi

HOW TO BREAK THE RULES OF BRAND DESIGN IN 10+8 EASY EXERCISES

Stefano Caprioli
Pietro Corraini

Edizioni Corraini

Design a trademark and a logo. Then take a sheet of paper, or an envelope, and print them on it. In addition to the mark and the logo, it is vital to choose a colour and a typeface you like.

And then use them for every application.
And then use them for every application.
And then use them for every application.
And then use them for every application.
And then use them for every application.
And then use them for every application.
And then use them for every application.
And then use them for every application.
And then use them for every application.
And then use them for every application.
And then use them for every application.
And then use them for every application.
And then use them for every application.
And then use them for every application.
And then use them for every application.
And then use them for every application.
And then use them for every application.
And then use them for every application.
And then use them for every application.
And then use them for every application.
And then use them for every application.
And then use them for every application.
And then use them for every application.
And then use them for every application.
And then use them for every application.
And then use them for every application.
And then use them for every application.
And then use them for every application.
And then use them for every application.
And then use them for every application.
And then use them for every application.
And then use them for every application.
And then use them for every application.
And then use them for every application.
And then use them for every application.
And then use them for every application.
And then use them for every application.
And then use them for every application.
And then use them for every application.
And then use them for every application.
And then use them for every application.
And then use them for every application.
And then use them for every application.
And then use them for every application.
And then use them for every application.

THE   IN

TY PRO

IS OBS

DENTI-
OGRAM
OLETE

CONSORTIUM OF SHEPHERDS

Trademark and logo for a group of shepherds and local cheese-makers.

consortium of shepherds

Trademark and logo for a group of shepherds and
local cheese-makers.

Consortium of shepends

*Trademark and logo for a group of shepherds and
local cheese-makers.*

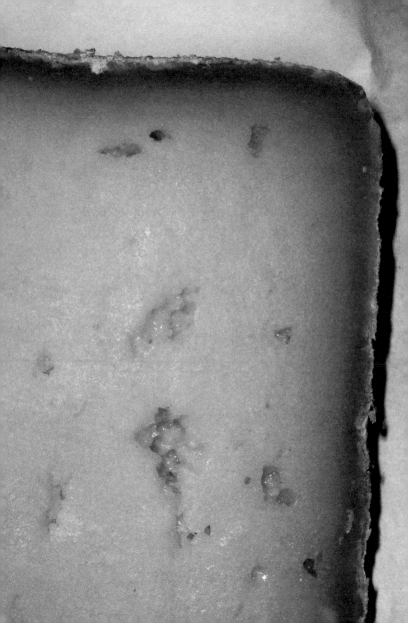

The same type of cheese can take on a variety of tastes and flavours depending on the place and time when it is made and matured. But it is always the same type of cheese.

So how can we distinguish them?

By the shape of the cheese **or by the manufacturing process?**

Starting
with
some raw
materials
and utensils,
one sets a
goal and
adopts a
method.

The very same process produces results that are similar **but always different from each other.**

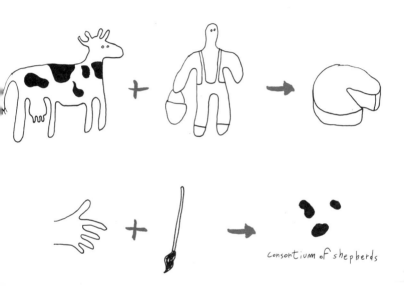

consortium of shepherds

The language used for the consortium of shepherds must be as close as possible to the way the cheese is made.

The process is nothing but a sequence of actions and every action can be broken down as follows:

INTENTION ──

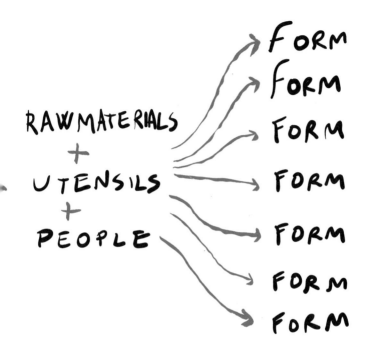

RAW MATERIALS
+
UTENSILS
+
PEOPLE

FORM
FORM
FORM
FORM
FORM
FORM
FORM

The results may in turn be incorporated, as raw materials, into other processes for obtaining products of even greater complexity.

TRADEMARK

Intention
make as many marks as you like,
in whatever manner you like, on a
sheet of paper.
Raw materials
black tempera on any kind of paper
or other type of support according
to whatever is required.
Utensils
round-tipped brush.
People
a graphic designer or any shepherd
in the consortium.

CONSORTIUM OF SHEPHERDS

LOGO

Intention
reproduce the words, any way you like: lower case, upper
case, small caps, italics; the important thing is that the
designer thinks it is legible.
Raw materials
any sheet of paper.
Utensils
fine-tipped black marker pen.
People
a graphic designer or any shepherd in the consortium.

USES OF TRADEMARK AND LOGO

Intention
reproduce the trademark and logo, either separately or together, with no particular instructions about their composition; it is important that the colours chosen are legible against any background.

Raw materials
original or digitalised trademark and logo, any type of paper or support and application according to whatever is required.

Utensils
scanner, air-brush, printers, photocopiers, video.

People
a graphic designer or any shepherd.

Consortium of Shepherds

PATTERN

Intention
fill a surface with logos all of
the same colour, mantaining an
inclination of 45°.

Raw materials
as many logos, sheets of paper,
or any other kind of support, as
possible.

Utensils
fine-tipped black marker to
create the pattern, scanner
and air-brush programmes
for changing the colour of
the writing in its various
applications.

People
the more graphic designers or
shepherds that pass the marker
pen around, the better.

FOOD PACKAGING

Intention
to reproduce the pattern of "Consortium of
shepherds" on food-wrapping paper. The colour of
the pattern and paper must ensure it is legible.
Raw materials
pattern, food-wrapping paper.
Utensils
any page layout programme.
People
a different graphic designer each time.

1st PRINCIPLE OF UNPROGRAMMED IDENTITY

The trademark is the process.

An identity program defines and controls forms to achieve unique graphic results. The attributes of a trademark are designed once and for all, and if they are called into question then it is said that the identity program has been redesigned.

An unprogrammed identity defines and controls a process for obtaining a series of graphic results each different from the others but linked by genetic similarity. **In this respect recognizability works on a level not of form, but of the rules of the form's production.**

The unprogrammed identity handbook does not specify the forms of communication being produced, but only defines the processes producing them. **It is the job of the unprogrammed identity designer to rigorously set down the intentions, raw materials, utensils and people involved in every creative process, always stating the constraints and margins of freedom.** An unprogrammed identity can only be communicated in the form of instructions and examples.

Instructions and margins of freedom introduce two variables into the graphics project, **causality** and **randomness**, making an unprogrammed identity a set of specific methods producing results with **endless stylistic variations** which cannot be determined in advance.

Etymology of the word
trademark

A trademark is a sign printed
on something to define its
properties.
The word -*mark* derives from the
German *marka* meaning sign.
The word *sign* probably comes
from *secare* meaning to cut.
The etymology of the word *sign*
evokes an action or gesture.
The trademark is the process;
the form of the trademark is a
consequence of this process.

THE FORM OF THE TRADEMARK IS INDICATIVE OF THE PROCESS.

DRAW A BLACK CIRCLE

With a thin-tipped black marker trace
a number of circles on this page with a
radius more or less similar to those that
have already been drawn.

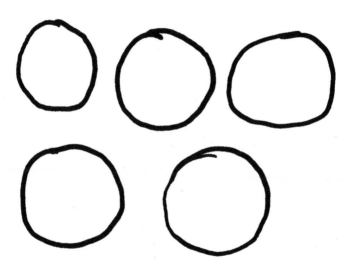

DRAW A CLOSED CURVE INSIDE ANOTHER CLOSED CURVE

With a fine-tipped black marker trace a closed curve inside each of the enclosed curves presented.

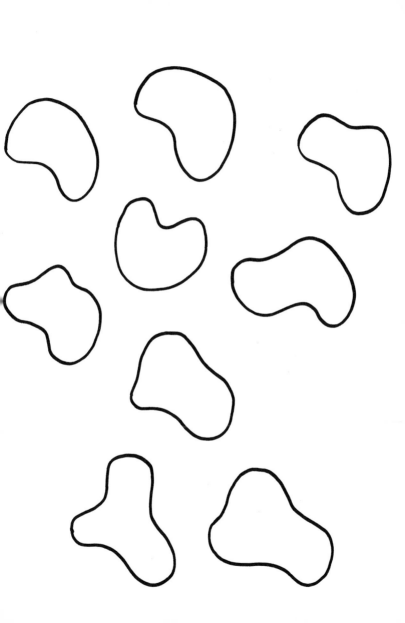

COLOUR IN THE SQUARE

Without taking your marker off the
page, if possible, quickly colour in the
square.

CONNECT THE DOTS

Use a fine-tipped marker to connect the
dots in any order you wish.

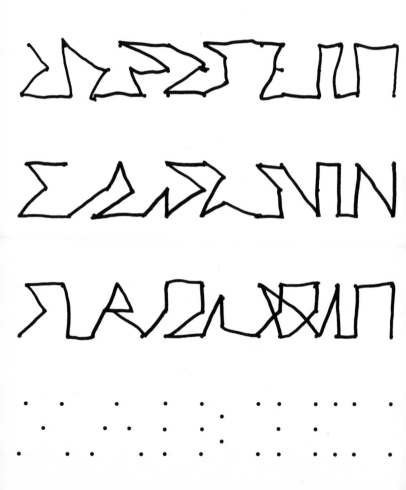

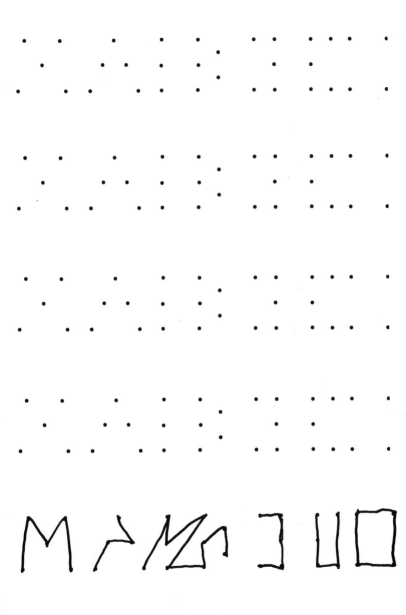

A trademark may
be two-dimensional
but represented
three-dimensionally,
like the writing on
a neon sign, or it
may be designed in
three dimensions
and **represented
from more than one
viewpoint.**

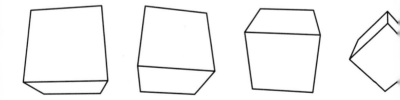

Let's assume our trademark is a geometric solid. Study it from various points of view of your choice: the important thing is to ensure that the entire trademark can be seen properly.

   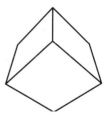

Although some versions may be better than others, you can always choose your favourite from among the possible forms.

Studying examples of a unprogrammed identity, **similar but always different from each other,** means altering how the trademark is perceived, making dynamic what was previously static and unchanging.
The dimension of time is added to that of space, and a **trademark applied today might be different tomorrow.**

Imagine a hypothetical trademark for a virtual community. Whenever the community gains a new member, another coloured dot will be placed inside a predetermined area.

Depending on the virtual community's popularity, the appearance of the trademark may alter any moment or may stay the same for months.

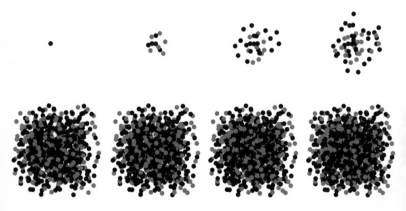

Introducing the dimension of time into a graphic design means giving the trademark its own vital essence.

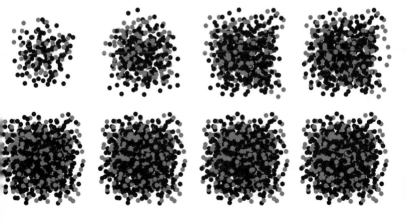

2nd PRINCIPLE OF UNPROGRAMMED IDENTITY

The processes involved in an unprogrammed identity may be classified in three ways:

delegating, sampling, making mistakes.

DELEGATING
graphic work to third
parties

SAMPLING
phenomena, collections
or bits of reality

MAKING MISTAKES
caused by the
machines or people
involved in the
trademark production
process

DELEGATING

Draw a flower. Draw a car. Draw a little house or stylised man.
Delegating means setting more or less precise rules and letting others produce the trademark as required.
The unprogrammed identity of the *consortium of shepherds* is the result of delegating. You can delegate the reproduction of a geometric figure or a simple drawing. You can delegate the composition of a text. You can delegate the layout of certain elements in space.
You can delegate to anyone: experts or not; graphic designers or shepherds;
women or computers.

SAMPLING

**Democratic trademark of
the Republic of Italy**

"Italy is a democratic Republic". The
trademark of the Republic of Italy must
represent all Italians: one at a time.

Patiently collect photos in profile of everyone
in Italy.

Create silhouettes from them and then put
different ones inside the current emblem.

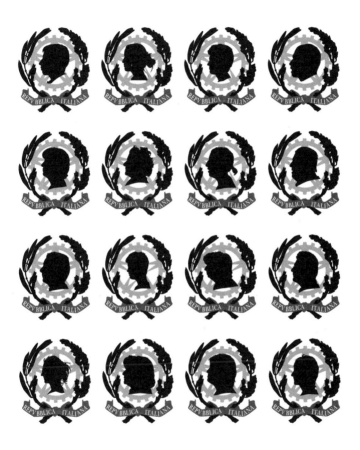

***Atlantide*, an unprogrammed identity for a search engine serving libraries.**

The job of a research engine like Google is to respond to key words entered by users with long lists of more or less pertinent results. *Atlantide* could be one of these search engines designed for handling a library's reference material. Whenever you need to compose the word *Atlantide*, open a randomly chosen book from those in a given library and scan an *A*. Close the book and pick up another; choose a *T* and scan it. Patiently and meticulously repeat the operation for the remaining letters *l, a, n, t, i, d* and *e*. If you like, you can also use the letters on the book's cover. The scans need to be made out in black and white.
At the end of this procedure, tidily replace all the books used on their proper shelves.

atlaNTidE

atlanTIDe

AtLanTide

AtLantide

atlanTIdE

aTLantiDe

atlanTIde

AtlAntiDE

aTLaNtidE

MAKING MISTAKES

A precise rule produces equally precise results, but with the interference of contingent factors it is possible to reduce control over the process. Introducing the possibility of mistakes into an abstract rule guarantees different outcomes.

Accidental bumps

Ask a seismologist or just any old expert on volcanoes or earthquakes to draw as straight a line as possible on a sheet of paper. When least expected, give them a nudge on the shoulder.

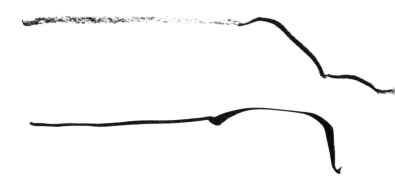

Lava, a centrifugal trademark

Reproduce the following trademark while seated on a washing machine during the spin cycle. It will help to rest the sheet of paper you are using on a rigid support, like for example a piece of cardboard, or you can even draw the trademark on a piece of tracing paper, but this should only be attempted by beginners.

Draw a square with your eyes closed

Draw a square of any size with a soft pencil, making sure to take the pencil off the paper after completing each side. It is advised to remove the pencil for at least five seconds, flicking it in the air, or making random or even pointless gestures.

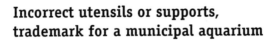

Incorrect utensils or supports, trademark for a municipal aquarium

Reproduce the following drawing using a watercolour and absorbent paper. The trademark should be painted in no more than two strokes.

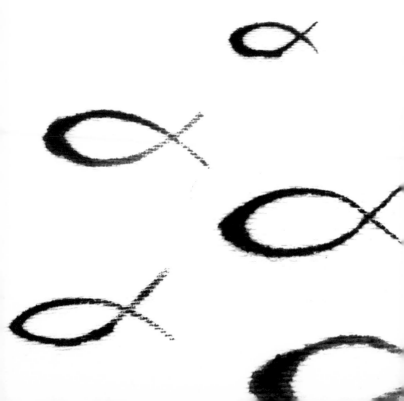

Scanner and electromagnetic interferences

Ask an expert in electromagnetism to generate, at their discretion, an electromagnetic field powerful enough to interfere with the scanning of the trademark for a hypothetical telecommunications campaign.

Unfortunately we do not know a good expert in electromagnetism.
Producing an unprogrammed identity also requires interdisciplinary skills.

Delegate, sample and make mistakes: deliberately acting along these lines positions you between order and chaos. The freedom or constraint imposed by the instructions provided, the amount of subjectivity or automation chosen, and the predictability of error can lead to more or less similar formal results, more or less close to the designer's expectations.

3rd PRINCIPLE OF UNPROGRAMMED IDENTITY

The amount of coordination in an unprogrammed identity depends on the control the designer has over the process.

In an unprogrammed identity everything not explicitly forbidden is actually possible.

The freer the processes, the more the forms will tend to evolve over time.

DRAW A CIRCLE WITH YOUR LEFT HAND
(DOES NOT APPLY TO THE LEFT-HANDED OR THE AMBIDEXTROUS!)

Take a fine-tipped black marker and use your left hand to draw some circles with more or less the same radius as those which have already been drawn.

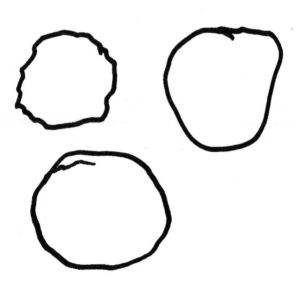

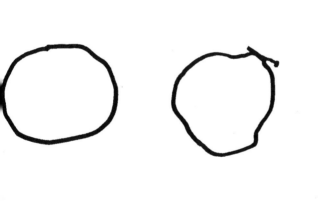

COLOUR IN THE SQUARE

Using a fine-tipped black marker quickly colour in the square with a continuous zig-zag line, following the direction shown in the example.

COLOUR IN THE SQUARE

Using a fine-tipped black marker quickly
colour in the square with a zig-zag line
in any direction you wish.

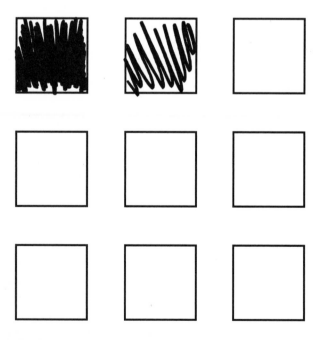

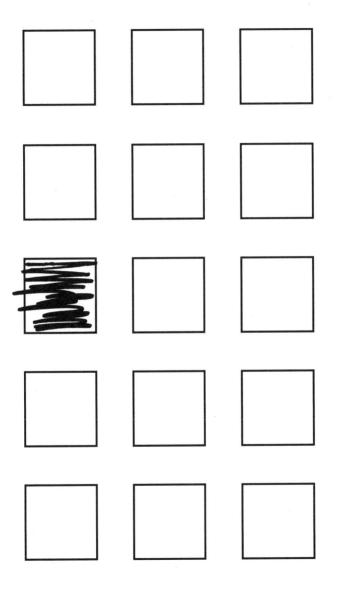

COLOUR IN THE SQUARE

Using a black marker
quickly colour in the square.

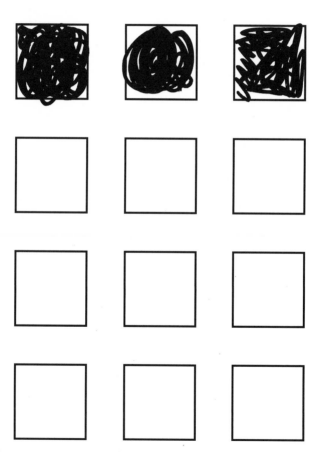

COROLLARY TO THE 3rd PRINCIPLE OF UNPROGRAMMED IDENTITY

An identity program is nothing but a subset of an unprogrammed identity.

Trademark for a computer firm

The logo is created geometrically over a grid containing alignments, spaces and radii of curvature for the construction of individual letters. The ratio of the base of the logo to its height is 5:1. All the enlargements and reductions must conform to this ratio.
The logo must be reproduced to the exact proportions indicated by the parameters of the grid.

To avoid visual interference of any kind with other graphic elements related to the logo, it is advisable to keep a free area equal to 10% of the length and 35% of the overall height of the logo.

This free area ensures the logo is always clear and easy to read.

The Management's permission is required if you wish to combine the logo with other trademarks or logos in unauthorised situations or settings.

The logo must never be:
- Altered in any way in terms of its lettering and composition
- An integral part of a text or address
- Used partly positively and partly negatively
- Used as a pattern
- Used against pattern backgrounds
- Used with shaded areas or three-dimensional letterforms
- Used with a frame

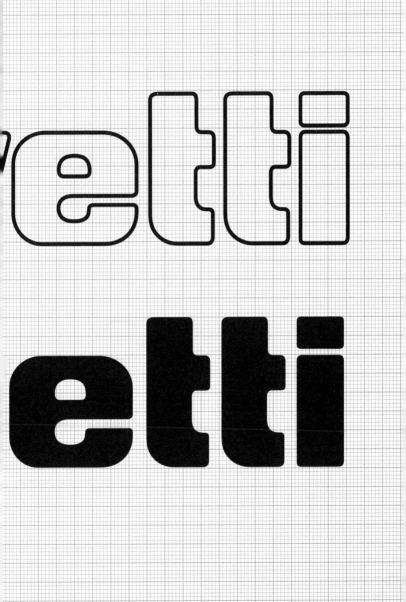

TOWARDS A MORE NATURAL LANGUAGE

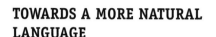

Like an identity
program, an
unprogrammed
identity is also
composed of a
trademark, logo,
colours and standard
type.

Unlike an identity program, however, an
unprogrammed identity involves reproducing
the trademark every time it is used. An
identity program defines the form of a
trademark, an unprogrammed identity
defines the production process. Re-thinking a
trademark along the lines of process involves a
basically genetic approach to graphic design.

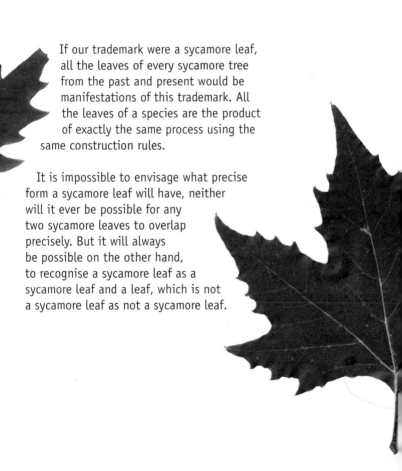

If our trademark were a sycamore leaf,
all the leaves of every sycamore tree
from the past and present would be
manifestations of this trademark. All
the leaves of a species are the product
of exactly the same process using the
same construction rules.

It is impossible to envisage what precise
form a sycamore leaf will have, neither
will it ever be possible for any
two sycamore leaves to overlap
precisely. But it will always
be possible on the other hand,
to recognise a sycamore leaf as a
sycamore leaf and a leaf, which is not
a sycamore leaf as not a sycamore leaf.

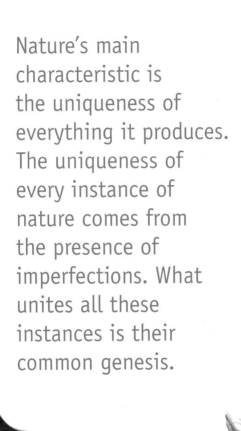

Nature's main characteristic is the uniqueness of everything it produces. The uniqueness of every instance of nature comes from the presence of imperfections. What unites all these instances is their common genesis.

Errata Corrige

at page 46 in stead of
women or computers
read
men, women, kids or computers

Stefano Caprioli, Pietro Corraini
**HOW TO BREAK THE RULES OF BRAND DESIGN
IN 10+8 EASY EXERCISES**

Thanks to Francesca Valsecchi, Laura Castelli, Stefano Mandato,
Giulio Ceppi, Beppe Finessi and Steven Guarnaccia.

Translation by Martyn John Anderson

First edition, April 2008

Printed in Italy by
Arti Grafiche Castello, Viadana (Mantova)
April 2008

Maurizio Corraini s.r.l.
Via Ippolito Nievo, 7/A
46100 Mantova
Tel. 0039 0376 322753
Fax 0039 0376 365566
e-mail: sito@corraini.com
www.corraini.com

ISBN 978-88-7570-164-2